SAUCES & DRESSINGS
THAT PUTS THE
ZING IN ANY MEAL

SAUCES & DRESSINGS THAT PUTS THE ZING IN ANY MEAL

CHEF FRANK OROFINO

authorHOUSE®

AuthorHouse™ LLC
1663 Liberty Drive
Bloomington, IN 47403
www.authorhouse.com
Phone: 1-800-839-8640

Published by AuthorHouse 02/21/2014

ISBN: 978-1-4918-6830-0 (sc)
ISBN: 978-1-4918-6829-4 (e)

GRANDMA AND GRANDPA

I remember the years gone by of growing up in my house with my Italian grandparents. They were the most gentleness and loving people. My grandfather came over from Italy many years ago. I remember my mother telling me stories about my grandfather being a carbon aria which is a policeman in Italy. As a young man my grandfather came over to America from Italy. Can you imagine all the people traveling from all parts of the world looking for a new start in what they called America? I could never imagine the faces and expressions on those seeing the symbol of freedom as they pass the Statue of liberty and being received at Rickers Island. Can you imagine what they were thinking? Coming off the boats and seeing thousands of people like them waiting to come into America. Many people always thought that the word WOP was considered a name strictly for Italians, but anyone coming over from any part of the word was considered a WOP which meant With out Passport. These people were hulled into a large building and waiting on line for weeks to get into America. I could never imagine what the strain was on these people on where they would go after they entered America. Most of the immigrants stayed closed to New York and New Jersey.

Many small areas became the settling places for many of these immigrants. This started many areas of Italian, Polish, Jewish and many other ethic groups in areas on the East Coast. All of these immigrants brought over with them their ethic foods that were instrumental in the American culture to this day. The foods of the immigrants were plain and simple but had the culture and taste of their home land. It must have been very hard for these people coming over from other countries not be able to speak English. But they were comfortable in their small areas where they all lived together. As time progressed they found a way to speak English and to develop into the Americas as a strong value to the Americas.

They brought over with them many skills to give America a strong versatile building block that would emerge as a strong power in the world. The knowledge of farming, carpentry, iron work, and many more drove the Americas into a building block that molded all groups into one. Yes there were conflicts that arose, but soon each knew that together they were contributing to the building of strong communities.

We the people of the Americas owe all ethic groups our strong up bringing and family values. As the ethic groups who came over from all parts of the world they found themselves incorporating with their ethic groups that were already here in America.

This book is dedicated to the two most important people in my life. My grandmother and grandfather Massaro. Through the years these gentle people taught me the meaning of life, responsibility and the most important thing is the love of the family. Family to my grandparents meant everything; they kept us together as a family and meet all good and bad moments as a family. The love they gave to all of us was undying, sincere and expressed.

So grandma and grandpa god bless you, as the tomb stone reads-ALWAYS IN OUR HEARTS. This is in remembrance of both of you

THE LATER YEARS

Well let's get into my later years, did my time in the military, Air Force. Stationed in England and all over the world at times. When I was discharged from the service I went to work with my father-in-law in his machine shop for awhile, as I was delivering parts to a company I came across an ad on Tonnelle Ave by Crown Cork and Seal for a mechanic. So that next day I applied and took the test and started the next week. This company made steel cans for the beverage industry. After about 2 years I was laid off but fortunately my supervisor also left and went to work for another can company and hired me. 7 years later I was offered a job in Ohio to build a can plant for a beer that was Stroh's. After different companies bought the plant after 41 years of going through different companies I finally retired from the can industry.

My passion has always been cooking, I was thought at an early age by my grandmother in the art of old world Italian cooking. The cooking came from the region of Naples and Caserta.

I always wanted to know if my food was good enough for customers in a restaurant. There was a restaurant in Fremont that I thought I could apply for and cook. I met the Chef, Chef Lou would talk to me and said, Frank cook me one of your dishes. So I made him veal in a white wine sauce with capers and wild mushrooms.

He seemed to enjoy it because when he was finished he had asked me when you can start. That was so exciting to me that he enjoyed my dish. What started out to be part time 2 days a week because I did have my full time job became 4 nights a week including Friday and Saturday nights?

My friends from work came to the restaurant to enjoy the food I served and Chef Lou gave me the freedom to explore different ways to prepare the food.

A couple of years later the restaurant closed but my passion for cooking never stopped. I cooked for neighbors and my fellow workers. Later in life I was at a truck restaurant getting a steak sandwich and I ran into a friend of mine. He introduced me to a chef that was opening up a new restaurant in town. I was the first one to be at his restaurant Friday night. Every since I came to his restaurant every Friday night. We became very close and helped him out in the morning with prepping. After that he was offered a new restaurant in downtown Sandusky. He and I worked on the restaurant getting it ready to open up. Jesse the chef taught me a lot about restaurant business and the way to run and operate a restaurant. The recipes we developed are still being served at the restaurant.

CONTENTS

I DEDICATE THIS BOOK TO MY LOVING WIFE WHO HAS BEEN THERE FOR ME IN THE CREATION OF THIS COOK BOOK AND THROUGH MY LIFE.

I LOVE YOU MORE

FRANK

ALMOND CREAM

½ CUP ALMONDS

½ CUP ROASTED GARLIC

ADD 2 QUARTS WATER

ADD 1 TBL CHICKEN BASE

BRING ALL INGREDIENTS TO A BOIL SUMMER UNTIL ALMONDS ARE TENDER ABOUT 30 MINUTES

ADD THE GARLIC AND ALMONDS IN THE BLENDER ALONG WITH 1 CUP OF THE LIQUID FROM THE POT AND THE 5 SLICES OF DAY OLD BREAD UNTIL SMOOTH. IF MORE LIQUID IS NEEDED ADD 1 CUP AT A TIME UNTIL SMOOTH BUT NOT LIQUIDY

YOU CAN USE ANY BREAD TO THIS MIXTURE SO LONG IT IS STALE

YOU CAN DRIZZLE THIS ON EITHER SQUASH OR TOMATO BISQUE SOUP

APPLE AIOLI

1 CUP MAYO

1 APPLE CORDED, PEELED AND DICED

JUICE OF 1 LEMON

1 TEASPOON OF DIJON MUSTARD

1 TEASPOON OF BROWN SUGAR

PUREE ALL INGREDIENTS IN BLENDER UNTIL SMOOTH AND CREAMY.

SERVE THIS ON TOP OF A BEET OR APPLE SALAD

APPLE TRUFFLE HONEY

¼ CUP CALVADOS LIQUIOR

½ CUP APPLE CIDER **(NOT APPLE VINEGAR)**

1/2 CUP HONEY

1 TEASPOON KOSHER OR SEA SALT

½ TEASPOON TRUFFLE OIL

SIMMER ALL INGREDIENTS TO INCORPORATE FLAVORS FOR 5 MINUTES WHILE MIXING CONSTANTLY STIR. REMOVE FROM HEAT AND LET COOL BEFORE SERVING.

THIS CAN BE DRIZZLED ON EITHER FISH OR PORK DISHES

ARUGULA PESTO

2 CUPS PACKED FRESH ARUGULA

1/2 TABLESPOON MINCED GARLIC

1/8 TEASPOON KOSHER OR SEA SALT

1/8 TEASPOON BLACK PEPPER

1/2 CUP OLIVE OIL

1 TABLESPOONS TOASTED PINE NUTS

½ CUP FRESHLY GRATED PARMESAN CHEESE

PREPARE AN ICE BATH IN A LARGE BOWL AND BRING A LARGE POT OF WATER TO A BOIL. PUT THE ARUGULA IN A LARGE SIEVE AND PLUNGE IT INTO BOILING WATER. BLANCH FOR ABOUT 15 SECONDS REMOVE AND PUT IT IN THE COLD WATER BATH STIR SO IT COOLS AS FAST AS POSSIBLE.

SQUEEZE THE WATER OUT OF THE ARUGULA WITH YOUR HANDS UNTIL IT IS VERY DRY. ROUGHLY CHOP THE ARUGULA AND PUT IN A BLENDER. ADD THE GARLIC SALT AND PEPPER TO TASTE THE OLIVE OIL AND THE PINE NUTS. BLEND FOR ABOUT 30 SECONDS. ADD THE CHEESE AND PULSE TO COMBINE.

SERVE AT ROOM TEMPERATURE. **DO NOT HEAT**

YOU CAN SUBSTITUE FRESH BASIL OR MINT IF YOU PREFER OR ANY COMBINATION OF HERBS

SERVE ON ANY PASTA

AVOCADO GREEN GODDESS DRESSING

1 AVOCADO PEELED AND PITTED

½ CUP MAYONNAISE

1 ANCHOVY FILET

1 TABLESPOONS CHOPPED GREEN ONIONS

1/2 TABLESPOON LEMON JUICE

1 CLOVE GARLIC CHOPPED

¼ TEASPOON KOSHER OR SEA SALT

1/8 TEASPOON BLACK PEPPER

COMBINE ALL INGREDIENTS IN A BLENDER OR FOOD PROCESSOR UNTIL SMOOTH AND CREAMY

SERVE ON ANY SALAD THAT YOU ARE MAKING

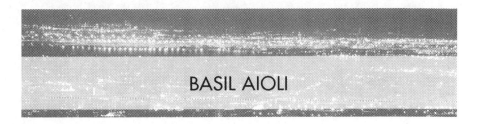

BASIL AIOLI

1 CUP MAYO

1 CUP BASIL LEAVES ONLY **(NO STEMS)**

1 TSP CHOPPED GARLIC

JUICE AND ZEST OF 1 LEMON

1 ANCHOVY

PUT INGREDIENTS IN BLENDER AND BLEND UNTIL SMOOTH. REFRIGERATE IMMEDIATELY AFTER BLENDING TO HOLD COLOR. **TO SERVE** REMOVE FROM REFRIGERATE AND LET STAND AT ROOM TEMPERATURE FOR 15 MINUTES

CAN BE USED AS A SALAD DRESSING OR TOP ON MEATS

BASIL/BUTTERMILK DRESSING

1 CUP BUTTERMILK

½ CUP MAYO

½ CUP BASIL LEAVES **(NO STEMS)**

4 CLOVES GARLIC

½ TABLESPOON WHITE VINEGAR

½ TEASPOON KOSHER OR SEA SALT

½ TEASPOON WHITE PEPPER

COMBINE ALL INGREDIENTS IN FOOD PROCESSOR AND BLEND UNTIL SMOOTH.

CAN BE USED ON ANY SALAD THAT YOU WANT TO MAKE.

BBQ SAUCE

2 CUPS CHERRY DOCTOR PEPPER

4 OZS CHERRY PRESERVE

1 TSP GARLIC POWDER

1 TSP ONION POWDER

1 TEASPOON KOSHER OR SEA SALT

½ TEASPOON WHITE PEPPER

1/2 TEASPOON SIRACHO

1/8 CUP WESTERSHIRE SAUCE

1/2 TEASPOON DIJON MUSTARD

PUT ALL INGREDIENTS IN A SAUCE PAN AND REDUCE BY HALF. REMOVE FROM HEAT AND LET COOL. STORE IN REFRIGERATOR.

CAN BE USED TO BAST RIBS, PORK LOINS, CHICKEN, STEAKS. CAN ALSO BE USED AS A DIPPING SAUCE.

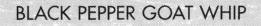

BLACK PEPPER GOAT WHIP

3 OZ GOAT CHEESE

3 OZ CREAM CHEESE

3 OZ CRÈME FRAICHE

1 TABLESPOON SHERRY VINEGAR

1 TABLESPOON WHITE PEPPER

1/2 TEASPOON KOSHER OR SEA SALT

WHIP UNTIL LIGHT AND FLUFFY IN A HAND HELD MIXER.

CAN BE USED ON A BEET SALAD, APPLE SALAD OR ANY OTHER SALADS THAT YOU MAKE.

BLACKBERRY AIOLI

½ CUP BLACKBERRIES

½ CUP RED WINE

½ CUP PORT WINE

2 LARGE SHALLOTS MINCED FINE

6 CLOVES ROASTED GARLIC

½ TEASPOON SALT

1/8 TEASPOON WHITE PEPPER

PUT ON MEDIUM HEAT REDUCE BY HALF, PUT IN BLENDER UNTIL MIXED THEN STRAIN THRU STRAINER

ADD 2 CUPS MAYO ADD SALT AND PEPPER AND MIX TOGETHER BY HAND.

SERVE ON PORK DISHES AND ALSO ON DUCK BREASTS AND DUCK LEGS.

BLOODY MARY SAUCE

½ CUP KETCHUP

1 RIPE TOMATO

1 CELERY STALK COARSELY CHOPPED

½ ONION COURSELY CHOPPED

2 TABLESPOONS HORSE RADISH

JUICE OF 1 LEMON

2 TEASPOONS TABASCO SAUCE

1 TABLESPOON WORCESTERSHIRE SAUCE

1 OZ VODKA **(NONE FLAVOR)**

1 TEASPOON CELERY SEED SPICE

½ TEASPOON KOSHNER OR SEA SALT

½ TEASPOON WHITE PEPPER

COMBINE ALL INGREDIIENTS IN FOOD PROCESSOR AND LEAVE CHUNKY

SERVE WITH SHRIMP, CRAB OR LOBSTER OR ANY OTHER SEAFOOD AS A COCKTAIL SAUCE.

BLUE CHEESE DRESSING

1 ½ CUPS MAYO

¼ CUP BUTTER MILK

1/2 TABLESPOON WORCESTERSHIRE SAUCE

JUICE AND ZEST OF 1 LEMON

1 1/2 CUPS BLUE CHEESE

1/4 CUP CRÈME FRISCH

COMBINE ALL INGREDIENTS BY HAND WITH WISK

SERVE AS A SALAD DRESSING WITH ANY LETTUCE, BEETS OR ANY SALAD DESIGH YOU COME UP WITH

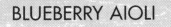

BLUEBERRY AIOLI

1 TEASPOON KOSHER OR SEA SALT

1 CUP BLUEBERRIES

5 CLOVES BLANCHED GARLIC **(BLANCHED GARLIC IN HOT WATER FOR 10 MINUTES)**

1 SHALLOT CHOPPED

1 TEASPOON WHITE PEPPER

1 TABLESPOON BUTTER

1 TABLESPOON BEEF OR VEAL BASE

1/4 CUP PORT WINE

¼ CUP RED WINE

REDUCE INGREDIENTS UNTIL THICK AND SYRUPERY. PUT IN FOOD PROCESSOR OR BLENDER WITH 1 CUP OF MAYO UNTIL SMOOTH.

SERVE OVER PORK CHOPS, LAMB CHOPS EVEN FISH.

BLUEBERRY AND PORT DRESSING

1 CUP PORT WINE

½ PINT BLUEBERRIES

¼ CUP SUGAR

 PUREE ALL INGREDIENTS IN BLENDER AND STRAIN. THEN PUT IN SAUCE PAN OVER MEDIUN HEAT AND REDUCE BY HALF.

SERVE AS A DRESSING OVER BEET SALAD WITH MICRO GREENS AND RED ONIONS.

CAESAR SALAD DRESSING

1 CUP OLIVE OIL

½ TEASPOON DIJON MUSTARD

2 ANCHOVIES

1/8 TEASPOON WHITE PEPPER

½ TABLESPOON WORCESTER SAUCE

JUICE OF 1 LEMON

1 EGG YOLK

COMBINE ALL INGREDIENTS IN BLENDER AND BLEND UNTIL SMOOTH.

SERVE OVER ROMAINE LETTUCE OR AND LETTUCE OF YOUR CHOSING.

CAESAR SALAD DRESSING

1 HEAD ROMANO LETTUCE

2 ANCHOVIES

1 TABLESPOON DIJON MUSTARD

1 EGG YOLK

1/4 TABLESPOON KOSHER OR SEA SALT

½ TABLESPOON BLACK PEPPER

JUICE OF 2 LEMONS

1 CUP GRATED PARMESAN CHEESE

TAKE THE HEAD OF LETTUCE AND RIP BY HAND PIECES INTO ½ INCH SIZES WITHOUT THE CORE AND PUT IN COLD WATER. REMOVE LETTUCE FROM WATER AND DRAIN THE LETTUCE IN WRAPED CLOTHS OR PAPER TOWELS UNTIL DRY.

TAKE THE REST OF THE INGREDIENTS EXCEPT FOR THE CHEESE AND PROCESS IN BLENDER UNTIL SMOOTH. PUT LETTUCE IN A LARGE BOWL AND ADD THE DRESSING AND MIX WELL TOP WITH THE GRATED CHEESE

YOU CAN SUBSITUTE ANY LETTUCE YOU DESIRE.

CARROT PUREE

3 LARGE CARROTS PEELED AND CHOPPED

1/2 TABLESPOON WHITE PEPPER

1/2 TABLESPOON KOSHER SALT

1/2 TABLESPOON SPICE MIX

1/2 CUP CHICKEN STOCK

¼ CUP HEAVY CREAM

COOK CARROTS IN WATER UNTIL SOFT AND TENDER. DRAIN CARROTS AND PUT IN BLENDER WITH THE REST OF THE INGREDIENTS PUREE UNTIL SMOOTH.

SERVE ON THE SIDE WITH ANY PORK DISH, OR FISH DISH.

CAULIFLOWER SOUP

1 TSP CHICKEN BASE

2 TBL LOBSTER BASE

2 CUPS CUT CAULIFLOWER

1 SLICE OF COOKED BACON

3 SPRINGS TYME

2 GARLIC GLOVES

1 SHALLOT

2 CUPS MILK

1 CUP HEAVY CREAM

½ TSP SALT

½ TSP WHITE PEPPER

1 LB LOBSTER **MEAT (CAN BE PURCHASED AT GROCERY STORE)**

SIMMER ALL INGREDIENTS IN SAUCE PAN FOR 20-30 MINUTES UNTIL CAULIFLOWER IS TENDER. DISCARD THE TYME. PUREE IN BLENDER UNTIL SMOOTH WHEN SERVING TOP WITH LOBSTER MEAT GARNISH WITH DEEP FRYED GARLIC ROOT.

SERVE HOT

CHARCOALED SCALLION RANCH

1 TABLESPOON RANCH SEASONING MIX **(ANY BRAND)**

1 TABLESPOON WATER

1/2 CUP BUTTERMILK

1/2 CUP MAYO

1 BUNCH (6) STALKS OF GRILLED GREEN ONION

PUT IN BLENDER BLEND TOGETHER UNTIL SMOOTH

TAKE 6 STALKS OF SCALLIONS AND GRILLED FOR ABOUT 10-15 MINUTES UNTIL THE GREEN PART STARTS TO BURN. ADD THE SCALLIONS TO THE ABOVE INGREDIENTS IN THE BLENDER.

SERVE AS A DRESSING ON ANY SALAD YOU CHOSE.

CHARRED TOMATO PESTO

1 CUP ROASTED TOMATOES IN JAR **(AVAILABLE AT ALL GROCERY STORES)**

¼ CUP SLICED ALMONDS

1 ANCHOVY **(NO OIL)**

1/4 TEASPOON DRYED ORGANO

1/2 TEASPOON STEAK SEASONING

½ TEASPOON CRUSHED RED PEPPER FLAKES

¼ CUP PARSLEY LEAVES

¼ CUP FRESH GARLIC MINCED

¼ TSP WHITE PEPPER

1/2 TEASPOON RED WINE VINEGAR

1/8 TEASPOON KOSHER OR SEA SALT

COMBINE ALL INGREDIENTS IN FOOD PROCESSOR. LEAVE CHUNCKY.

CAN BE SERVED ON PASTA, CAN BE SERVED ON ITALIAN AS AN APPETIZER OR AS A DIP WITH CRACKERS OR CHIPS.

CHESTNUT PUREE

1 CUP ROASTED CHESTNUTS

1 CUP CHICKEN STOCK

2 SPRIGS TYME

1 CLOVE GARLIC

COMBINE INGREDIENTS IN SAUCE PAN AND SIMMER FOR 20 MINUTES UNTIL CHESTERNUTS ARE TENDER. DISCARD TYME SPRIGS AND SAVE THE COOKING LIQUID. PUREE MIXTURE ADDING ½ CUP HEAVY CREAM. IF TOO THICK AND SOME OF THE COOKING LIQUID.

SERVE ON THE SIDE WITH DUCK BREAST OR CHICKEN BREAST.

CHIMICHURRI SAUCE

½ TEASPOON RED PEPPER FLAKES

1 TABLESPOON GARLIC PUREE

½ CUP OREGANO FRESH LEAVES

1 CUP PARSLEY LEAVES

6 THINLY SLICED DILL PICKLES

JUICE AND ZEST OF 1 LEMON

½ TEASPOON KOSHER SALT

½ TEASPOON WHITE PEPPER

½ CUP OLIVE OIL

PUT IN FOOD PROCESSOR- **LEAVE CHUNKY**

SERVE AS A CONDIMENT FOR PORK OR VEAL DISHES.

CHIPOTIE GLAZE

7 OZS CHIPOTLE CHILLIES IN ADOBO SAUCE **(CAN BE PURCHASED IN ANY GROCERY STORE)**

1 CUP PURE HONEY

½ CUP RICE WINE VINEGAR

COMBINE ALL INGREDIENTS IN A BLENDER AND PROCESS UNTIL SMOOTH.

CAN BE USED WHILE BARBARQUING ANY MEAT OR SEAFOOD ON THE GRILL.

CHIVE OIL

1 CUP CHIVES

1CUP OLIVE OIL

½ TSP SALT

¼ TSP WHITE PEPPER

PUREE ALL INGREDIENTS IN BLENDER THEN STRAIN THROUGH CHEESE CLOTH.

CAN BE USED TO DECORATE ANY DISH

CILANTRO LIME BUTTER

¼ STICK UNSALTED BUTTER

½ CUP CHOPPED CILANTRO (**LEAVES ONLY)**

ZEST AND JUICE OF 2 LIMES

1 TEASPOON KOSHER OR SEA SALT

¼ TEASPOON BLACK PEPPER

COMBINE ALL INGREDIENTS IN FOOD PROCESSOR OR BLENDER UNTIL SMOOTH.

CAN BE PUT ON TOP OF FISH, PORK, STEAK AFTER IT IS COOKED.

CITRUS VINEGARETTE

JUICE AND ZEST OF 1 LEMON- 1 ORANGE & 2 LIMES

1 CUP OF BLENDED OLIVE OIL

1 TABLESPOON SUGAR

½ TABLESPOON KOSHER OR SEA SALT

MIX ALL INGREDIENTS IN A BOWL WITH A WISK.

CAN BE PUT ON ANY TYPE OF GREENS OR FRUIT SALAD WITH GREENS.

CLAMS IN ORANGE AND BEER SAUCE

1 DOZ CHERRY STONE CLAMS

4 TABLESPOONS OLIVE OIL

2 CLOVES GARLIC FINELY CHOPPED

ZEST AND JUICE OF 1 WHOLE ORANGE

1 WHOLE ORANGE SECTIONED

1 SHALLOT THINLY SLICED

½ CUP PARSLEY LEAVES **(NO STEMS)**

2 TABLESPOONS CRÈME FRIES

1 (12)OZ BOTTLE BEER **(LAGER)**

IN A SAUCE PAN ADD OLIVE OIL AND CUT UP GARLIC AND THINLY SLICED SHALLOTS. AFTER A FEW MINUTES ADD THE CLAMS COOK FOR A FEW MINUTES UNTIL THEY ALL OPEN UP. THEN ADD A LAGER BEER COVER AND SIMMER UNTIL CLAMS OPEN UP. **(DISCARD ANY CLAMS THAT DO NOT OPEN UP)** ADD THE SLICES, ZEST AND JUICE OF THE ORANGES. ALSO THE WHOLE LEAVES OF PARSLEY AND ADD 2 TABLESPOONS OF CRÈME FRISC

MAKE TOAST AND SPREAD GARLIC AIOLI PUT IN A SOUP DISH AND THEN ADD THE CLAMS THE BROTH THE ORANGES AND PARSLEY

NOTE: YOU CAN SUBSTITUTE MUSSELS AGAIN DISCARD ANY MUSSELS THAT DO NOT OPEN UP

COCONUT CRÈME FRAICH

1 CUP CRÈME FRAICH

1/2 CAN COCONUT MILK

1/2 TEASPOON KOSHER OR SEA SALT

1/2 TABLESPOON RED CURRY PASTE

BLEND ALL INGREDIENTS IN BLENDER UNTIL SMOOTH

REFRIGERATE.

CAN BE USED ON TOP OF COOKED SHRIMP, CRAB SALAD, LOBSTER SALAD.

COCONUT PEANUT BUTTER SAUCE

1 CAN COCONUT MILK

2 CUPS PEANUT BUTTER (**SMOOTH ONE**)

COOK BOTH OVER LOW HEAT FOR 30 MINUTES UNTIL THE PEANUTS ARE SOFT

PUT IN FOOD PROCESSOR WITH THE FOLLOWING

¼ CUP SOY SAUCE

1 TSP SESAME OIL

2 TBL BROWN SUGAR

1 CUP HOT WATER

1 TBL RICE WINE VINEGAR

PUT INTO BLENDER AND PUREE UNTIL SMOOTH

CAN BE USED AS A DIPPING SAUCE FOR AND TYPE OF SEAFOOD.

COFFEE RUB

1 CUP FINE BLACK PEPPER

2 CUP DECAF COFFEE

½ CUP KOSHER OR SEA SALT

MIX ALL INGREDIENTS TOGETHER BY HAND

CAN BE USED ON STEAKS, SEAFOOD, PORK AND VEAL.

COGNAC MAYO

¾ CUP MAYO

1 TABLESPOON GARLIC **(FINELY CHOPPED)**

3 TABLESPOONS PARMESAN CHEESE

1 TABLESPOON LEMON JUICE

2 TABLESPOONS COGNAC

COMBINE ALL INGREDIENTS IN A BOWL AND WISK UNTIL BLENDED.

CAN BE USED TO TOP THE OYSTERS WHEN MAKING OYSTERS ROCKERFELLER, BAKED CLAMS, STUFF LOBSTERS, AND CAN BE PUT ON TOP OF ANY FISH WHEN SERVING.

COLD POTATO SOUP

2 SHALLOTS CHOPPED FINE

1 POUND GOLDEN POTATOES

2 TABLESPOONS BUTTER

¼ TEASPOON OF KOSHER OR SEA SALT

3 SPRIGES TYME & 3 BUNCHES PARSLEY WRAPPED IN CHEESE CLOTH AND TIED

1 CUP HEAVY CREAM

¼ TEASPOON WHITE PEPPER

1 TEASPOON MINCED CHIVES

1 TABLESPOON SHERRY WINE

PEEL POTATOES, WASH THEM AND SLICE INTO ½ INCH PIECES. MELT BUTTER IN A SOUP PAN AND ADD THE SHALLOTS. COOK OVER LOW HEAT UNTIL SHALLOTS ARE SOFT ABOUT 3 MINUTES. DO NOT ALLOW SHALLOTS AND BUTTER TO GET BROWN. ADD 1 ½ QUARTS OF WATER AND BRING TO BOIL. THEN ADD 1 TABLESPOON OF SALT TO WATER THE HERBS IN CHEESE CLOTH AND THE POTATOES. COOK FOR ABOUT 25 MINUTES OR UNTIL POTATOES ARE SOFT. REMOVE THE CHEESE CLOTH OF HERBS. BLEND THE SOUP WELL. ADD THE HEAVY CREAM AND BLEND AGAIN. ADD THE SALT AND PEPPER.

ALLOW THE SOUP TO COOL AT ROOM TEMPERATURE AND THEN REFRIGERATE IT FOR AT LEAST 3 HOURS. PUT IN BOWL AND SPRINKLE WITH CHIVES AND DRIZZLE THE TOP OF THE SOUP WITH SHERRY WINE

LOBSTER/SHRIMP POOR BOY DRESSING

1 1/2 CUPS MAYO

1 LEMON JUICED

4 TABLESPOONS GRAIN MUSTARD

1 TABLESPOONS SRIRACHA

¼ RED ONION CHOPPED FINELY

1 1/2 TABLESPOONS CHOPPED DILL

COMBINES ALL INGREDIENTS IN FOOD PROCESSOR UNTIL SMOOTH.

CAN BE PUT ON ANY SEAFOOD SANDWICH, SALAD SEAFOOD SALAD OR SHRIMO COCKTAIL AS WELL AS CRAB OR LOBSTER COCKTAIL.

TOMATO BISQUE

½ CUP BACON

1 CUP ONION

1 CUP CELERY

1 CUP CARROTS

ALL ABOVE GETS ROUGH CHOP

SWEAT INGREDIENTS IN 5 OZ OF BUTTER UNTIL SOFT. THEN AFTER 5 MINUTES. ADD 5 OZ FLOUR TO FORM A ROUX. PUREE IN BLENDER 1 CANS #10 ITALIAN PLUM TOMATOES AND ADD TO POT ALONG WITH 2 CUPS OF WATER AND 1 TABLESPOON CHICKEN BASE.

SIMMER FOR 30 MINUTES STIRRING OCCASIONALLY. ADD THE FOLLOWING INGREDIENTS:

 1 TEASPOON KOSHER SALT

 1 TEASPOON BLACK PEPPER

 1 CUP HEAVY CREAM

 1 CUP CHOPPED BASIL

LET COOL THEN PUREE IN BLENDER UNTIL SMOOTH.

CRAB SOUP

½ CUP CHOPPED ONION

½ CUP CHOPPED RED PEPPER

½ CUP CELERY

COOK ALL INGREDIENTS IN 5 OZ OF UNSALTED BUTTER FOR 15 MINUTES OR UNTIL SOFT.

MAKE A ROUX WITH 5 OZS OF BUTTER AND 5 OZS OF FLOUR MIX TOGETHER AND ADD TO POT CONSTANTLY STIRRING FOR 5 MINUTES ON MEDIUM HEAT. THEN ADD THE FOLLOWING INGREDIENTS:

½ CUP SHERRY WINE

½ CUP WORCESTERSHIRE SAUCE

2 TABLESPOONS CRAB BASE

3 CUPS MILK

2 CUPS HEAVY CREAM

STIR CONSTANTLY ON MEDIUM HEAT FOR ABOUT 20 MINUTES SO BOTTOM OF POT DOES NOT BURN.

REMOVE FROM HEAT AND LET COOL. PUT MIXTURE IN BLENDER AND BLEND UNTIL SMOOTH.

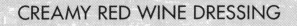

CREAMY RED WINE DRESSING

1/2 CUP SUGAR

1 TABLESPOON DRY SALAD DRESSING

1/2 TABLESPOON GARLIC POWDER

½ TEASPOON SALT

½ CUP RED WINE VINAGAR

½ CUP WATER

1/2 CUP MAYO

1/2 CUP BUTTERMILK

COMBINE ALL INGREDIENTS IN BOWL AND WISK BY HAND.

SERVE ON ANY SALAD THAT IS MADE WITH GREENS.

CUCUMBER MIGNONETTE

1 CUP RICE WINE VINEGAR

1 SHALLOT MINCED FINELY

1 INCH PIECE OF GINGER MINCED VERY FINELY

½ CUCUMBER PEELED, SEEDED AND MINCED FINELY

1 TABLESPOON SUGAR

½ TEASPOON WHITE PEPPER

COMBINE ALL INGREDIENTS IN A BOWL AND MIX BY HAND WITH WISK OR SPOON.

SERVE ON THE SIDE WITH FRESH RAW OYSTERS OR FRESH RAW CLAMS

CURRY VINAGARETTE

1 CUP MAYO

1/2 CAN COCONUT MILK

JUICE AND ZEST OF 2 LIMES

1 TABLESOON GINGER POWDER

1 TABLESPOON GARLIC POWDER

1 TEASPOON CURRY POWDER

1/2 TABLESPOON SOY SAUCE

1/2 TABLESPOON SIRACHA

1/4CUP PEANUT BUTTER **(NOT CHRUNCHY)**

1 TEASPOON WHITE PEPPER

¼ BANANA

1 TEASPOON SESAME OIL

1/2 TEASPOON TRUFFLE OIL

PUREE ALL INGREDIENTS IN BLENDER UNTIL SMOOTH.

SERVE ON TOP OF COOKED TUNA, FLOUNDER, SKATE, SORD FISH OR ANY OTHER FRESH FISH.

DARK RUM SAUCE

¼ CUP UNSALTED BUTTER

1 CUP BROWN SUGAR

¾ CUPS HEAVY CREAM

1 TABLESPOON VANILLA

1TABLESPOON KOSHER OR SEA SALT

1/4 CUP CHOCOLATE NIBS **(SWEET OR DARK)**

1 SHOT DARK RUM

MELT BUTTER, BROWN SUGAR CONSTANTLY MIXING UNTIL SMOOTH AND SUGAR CYSTALS HAVE DISAPPEARED.

BOIL GENTLY, STIRRING OCCESIONALLY UNTIL TEXTURE IS NOT GRITY

REMOVE FROM HEAT AND STIR IN CHOCOLATE UNTIL MELTED, STIR IN CREAM, VANILLA AND SALT.

MIX THROUGHLY.

CAN BE SERVED ON ANY ICE CREAM OR FRUIT CUP

DILL BUTTER

1/2 LB OF BUTTER **LET SET AT ROOM TEMPERATURE UNTIL SOFT**

1 LEMON **(ZEST ONLY)**

1/2 CUP CHOPPED DILL **(NO STEMS)**

1/4 TEASPOON SEA SALT

COMBINE ALL INGREDIENTS IN FOOD PROCESSOR. SPREAD BUTTER LENGTH WAYS ON PLASTIC WRAP. ROLL AND TWIST PLASTIC UNTIL A ROUND LOG IS ACHIEVED. STORE IN REFREGATOR.

CAN BE USED TO DRESS ANY MEATS OR SEAFOOD AFTER THEY ARE COOKED

FRENCH DRESSING

1/2 CUP SUGAR

1/2 CUP OLIVE OIL

1/2 CUP VINGAR

1/2 CAN TOMATO SOUP

1/8 TEASPOON WHITE PEPPER

1/2 TEASPOON KOSHER OR SEA SALT

1/2 TEASPOON GARLIC POWDER

1/2 TEASPOON PAPRIKA

1/2 TEASPOON OREGANO

1/2 TEASPOON A-1 STEAK SAUCE

1/2 TEASPOON WORSTERSHERE

COMBINE ALL INGREDIENTS IN BLENDER UNITL SMOOTH.

USE ON ANY SALAD MIXTURE WETHER IT BE LETTUCES OR BEETS OR FRUIT SALADS.

FRIED CALAMARI WITH A SPICY CHIPOTIE CHILI GLAZE AND PICKLED GINGER

1 POUNDS SQUID,RINSE IN COLD WATER THEN CUT INTO ¼ INCH RINGS

1 ½ CUPS ALL PURPOSE FLOUR

1 CUP PICKLE GINGER DICE IN SMALL PIECES **(GROCERY STORES WILL HAVE THIS IN A JAR)**

½ TEASPOON KOSHER OR SEA SALT

½ TEASPOON BLACK PEPPER

¼ CUP CHOPPED CHIVES

HEAT OIL TO 350 DEGREES. SEASON THE CALAMARI RINGS WITH SALT AND PEPPER. ROLL THE SQUID IN THE FLOUR TO COAT EVENLY. SHAKE OFF EXCESS FLOUR.

DEEP FRY AT UNTIL GOLDEN BROWN, ABOUT 2 MINUTES

DRAIN THE SQUID ON PAPER TOWELS AND COMBINE IN A BOWL WITH ONE CUP OF CHILI GLAZE, DICED PICKLED GINGER AND CHIVES.

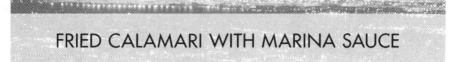

FRIED CALAMARI WITH MARINA SAUCE

1 POUNDS SQUID, RINSE IN COLD WATER THEN CUT INTO ¼ INCH RINGS

1 ½ CUPS ALL PURPOSE FLOUR

1 CUP MARINA SAUCE

½ TEASPOON KOSHER OR SEA SALT

½ TEASPOON BLACK PEPPER

HEAT OIL TO 350 DEGREES. SEASON THE CALAMARI RINGS WITH SALT AND PEPPER. ROLL THE SQUID IN THE FLOUR TO COAT EVENLY. SHAKE OFF EXCESS FLOUR.

DEEP FRY AT UNTIL GOLDEN BROWN, ABOUT 2 MINUTES

DRAIN THE SQUID ON PAPER TOWELS ARRANGE ON A DISH WITH A SIDE BOWL OF MARINA SAUCE FOR DIPPING.

MARINA SAUCE IS IN THE COOK BOOK OR USE YOUR FAVORITE SAUCE.

FRIED EGGPLANT

1 ITALIAN EGGPLANT

3 CUPS ANY BREADCRUMBS

3 CUPS VEGATABLE OIL

3 OUNCES OLIVE OIL

3 TABLESPOONS CAPERS

1 TABLESPOON KOSHER OR SEA SALT

¼ TEASPOON BLACK PEPPER

¼ CUP CHOPPED BASIL

¼ CUP SHAVED PARMESAN CHEESE

3 EGGS SCRAMBLED

CUT THE TOP OF THE EGGPLANT OFF, PEEL THE SKIN OFF THE EGGPLANT AND CUP THE BOTTOM OFF **(JUST A LITTLE PIECE).** THINLY SLICE THE EGGPLANT IN THE ROUND AND PLACE THE PIECES ON A COOKY SHEET. SPRINKLE THE EGGPLANT ON BOTH SIDES WITH THE SALT AND LET SIT FOR ABOUT 30 MINUTES.

WHILE YOU ARE WAITING SCRAMBLE THE EGGS IN A LARGE DISH. PUT THE BREAD CRUMBS IN A SEPARATE DISH ALSO.

NOW RINSE THE EGGPLANTS IN COLD WATER AND PAT DRY. HEAT UP THE VEGTABLE OIL IN A FRYING PAN. TAKE EACH PIECE OF EGGPLANT AND DIP IT FIRST IN EGG AND THEN IN BREAD CRUMBS COATING BOTH SIDES.

COOK IN FRYING PLAN ABOUT 3 MINUTES EACH SIDE AND THEN PLACE ON COOKY SHEET LINED WITH PAPER TOWEL TO DRAIN EXCESS OIL.

ARRANGE THE PIECES OF EGGPLANT ON A LARGE DISH. SPRINKLE WITH THE OLIVE OIL, CAPERS, BLACK PEPPER, BASIL AND SHAVED PARMASAN CHEESE.

GOAT CHEESE CRÈME FRIECH

1 CUP CRÈME FRISECH

1 1/2 TABLESPOONS GOAT CHEESE

COMBINE BOTH INGREDIENTS IN FOOD PROCESSOR UNTIL SMOOTH

GREEN GODDESS DRESSING

AFTER PREPARING THE CHARCOALED SCALLION RANCH RECEIPE BEFORE REMOVING FROM BLENDER ADD THE FOLLOWING INGREDIENTS:

1 AVACADO PEELED REMOVE SEED, AND CUT INTO CUBES

2 ANCHOVIES

JUICE AND ZEST OF 1 LEMON

COMBINE THE INGREDIENTS AND BLEND AGAIN UNTIL SMOOTH

HONEY/BACON DRESSING

½ CUP BACON GREASE

¼ CUP EXTRA VIRGIL OLIVE OIL

2 TABLESPOONS DIJON MUSTARD

¼ CUP HONEY

¼ CUP SHERRY VINGAR

BLEND ALL INGREDIENTS IN A BLENDER UNTIL SMOOTH.

LAMB MEATBALLS

1 LB LAMD CHOP MEAT

1 LB VEAL CHOP MEAT

1 LB PORK CHOP MEAT

3 WHOLE EGGS SCRAMBLED

2 CUPS ITALIAN BREAD CRUMBS

1 TABLESPOON KOSHER OR SEA SALT

1 TABLESPOON BLACK PEPPER

2 TABLESPOONS DRY BASIL

2 TABLESPOONS DRY ORGANO

2 TABLESPOONS DRY GARLIC POWDER

½ CUP WHOLE MILK

COMBINE ALL INGREDIENTS IN A LARGE MIXING BOWL BUT DO NOT OVER MIX. MIX INGREDIENTS FOR ABOUT 3 MINUTES VERY GENTLY.

ON A COOKY SHEET LINED WITH PARAMENT PAPER ROLL MIXTURE INTO A GOLF BALL SIZE BALL. COOK MEATBALLS IN A 350 DEGREE OVEN FOR 12-14 MINUTES.

YOU CAN SERVE THEM ANY WAY YOU WANT WITH ANY OF THE DRESSINGS IN THE BOOK

LEMON/ BASIL OIL

ZEST OF 1 LEMON

½ CUP BASIL LEAVES (NO STEMS)4 ROASTED GARLIC CLOVES

2 CUPS OLIVE OIL

BLEND ALL INGREDIENTS IN BLENDER UNTIL SMOOTH.

LEMON-PEA PUREE

2 CUPS FROZEN PEAS

1/2 CUP HEAVY CREAM

1 LEMON ZEST AND JUICE

½ TEASPOON KOSHER OR SEA SALT

½ TEASPOON WHITE PEPPER

HEAT INGREDIENTS IN A SAUCE PAN BRING TO A BOIL REMOVE FROM HEAT AND PUREE. PUT IN BLENDER AND PUREE. PUT IN CONTAINER IMMEDIATELY AND PUT IN REFRIGERATOR TO KEEP THE COLOR AND FRESHNESS.

LOBSTER SPICE

½ TABLESPOON MUSTARD SEED

½ TABLESPOON CORIANDER SEED

½ TABLESPOON FENNEL SEED

1 BAY LEAF

1/8 TEASPOON OF CAYENNE PEPPER

NOTE: FIRST THREE SEEDS HEAT IN A FRYING PAN ON MEDIUM HEAT FOR ABOUT 5 MINUTES OR UNTIL YOU AND SMELL THE HERBS DO NOT BURN

GRIND ALL INGREDIENTS IN COFFEE GRINDER UNTIL SMOOTH

MALT VINEGAR AIOLI

1 CUP MAYO

1/4 CUP BUTTERMILK

1/2 TABLESPOON BLACK PEPPER

1 TABLESPOONS GARLIC POWDER

3 TABLESPOONS MALT VIMEGAR

COMBINE ALL INGREDIENTS IN BLENDER UNTIL SMOOTH

MARINARA SAUCE

1 ONION SMALL DICE

2 TABLESPOONS MINCED GARLIC

1 ANCHOVY

1/2 CUP OLIVE OIL

1 ½ CUPS BASIL CHOPPED

1 (10 OZ) CAN PLUM TOMATO

COMBINE ALL INGREDIENTS EXCEPT THE BASIL AND PLUM TOMATOES IN A SAUCE PAN. SWEAT INGREDIENTS UNTIL TRANSLUCENT AND ANCHOVY HAS DISSOLVED. PUT PLUM TOMATOES AND BASIL IN POT AND SIMMER FOR 30 MINUTES. USE POTATO MASHER TO BREAKDOWN TOMATOES AS THE SAUCE IS COOKING. SIMMER FOR 30 MINUTES.

MISO DRESSING

1 TABLESPOON MISO

2 TEASPOON WORCESTERSHIRE SAUCE

2 TSP SESAME OIL

1 CUP OLIVE OIL

½ CUP APPLE CIDER VINEGAR

1 TABLESPOON DIJON MUSTARD

1 TABLESPOON HONEY

JUICE OF ½ LEMON

2 TEASPOONS GROUND GINGER

2 TEASPOONS ROASTED GARLIC PUREE

1 SHALLOT MINCED FINELY

COMBINE ALL INGREDIENTS IN BLENDER UNTIL SMOOTH.

MUSSELS IN WHITE WINE SAUCE

1 DOZEN MUSSELS CLEANED AND DEBEARDED

2 CLOVES CHOPPED GARLIC

4 TABLESPOONS OLIVE OIL

2 CUP WHITE WINE **(WHAT EVER KIND YOU DRINK)**

½ TEASPOON SALT

½ TEASPOON BLACK PEPPER

1 CUP CHERRY TOMATOES CUT IN HALF

¼ CUP PARSLEY **(NO STEMS)**

IN A PAN HEAT 4 TABLESPOONS OF OLIVE OIL ADD CHOPPED GARLIC, WHEN HEATED ADD THE MUSSELS AND COVER THE PAN WITH A LID. WHEN YOU SEE THE MUSSELS ARE STARTING OPENED UP ADD THE CUT CHERRY TOMATOES, 2 CUP OF WHITE WINE AND CHOPPED PARSLEY SALT AND PEPPER TO TASTE. COOK FOR ABOUT 4 MORE MINUTES OR UNTIL ALL THE MUSSELS ARE OPEN.

NOTE: DISCARD ANY MUSSELS THAT DO NOT OPEN SAME GOES FOR THE CLAMS IF YOU ARE SUBSTITUTING THEM

DEBEARDING MUSSELS: IF IT LOOKS LIKE THERE IS A BEARD ON THE MUSSELS, JUST PULL THE BEARD OFF FROM THE SHELL. NO NEED TO DO THIS TO THE CLAMS.

YOU CAN ALSO SUSTITUTE SHRIMP FOR THIS DISH

MUSSELS WITH MARINA SAUCE

1 DOZEN MUSSELS CLEANED AND DEBEARD

2 CLOVES CHOPPED GARLIC

4 TABLESPOONS OLIVE OIL

2 CUPS MARINA SAUCE

½ TEASPOON KOSHER OR SEA SALT

½ TEASPOON BLACK PEPPER

¼ CUP PARSLEY LEAVES **(NO STEMS)**

IN A SAUCE PAN ADD 2 TABLESPOONS OF OLIVE OIL LET HEAT ADD THE CHOPPED GARLIC TO PAN ADD MUSSELS AND COVER THE PAN WITH A LID. WHEN MUSSELS ARE FULLY OPENED UP AND MARINA SAUCE, PARSLEY, SALT AND BLACK PEPPER

YOU CAN USE THE SAME RECEIPE WHEN COOKING CLAMS. THE CLAMS JUST SCRUB THE OUTSIDE SHELL IN COLD WATER. THERE IS NO BEARD TO THE CLAMS

FOR THE MARINA SAUCE FOLLOWING THE RECEIPE IN THE BOOK FOR THE MARINA SAUCE.

YOU CAN SUBSTITUTE SHRIMO FOR THIS DISH

MUSTARD SAUCE

½ QUART HEAVY CREAM

¼ CUP WHOLE GRAIN MUSTARD

1 TABLESPOON MINCED SHALLOTS

¼ CUP WHITE WINE

SIMMER ON LOW TEMPERATURE UNTIL REDUCED BY HALF. WHEN COOL PUT IN BLENDER AND BLEND UNTIL SMOOTH.

CAN BE SERVED AS A DIPPING SAUCE FOR SHRIMP, LOBSTER, AND CRAB.

ROMESCO SAUCE

2 ROASTED PEPPERS

½ CUP SLICED ALMONDS

½ CUP ROASTED TOMATOES IN JAR **(CAN BE PURCHASED AT ANY GROCERY** STORE)

1 ANCHOVY

1 TSP SALT

½ TEASPOON WHITE PEPPER

1 TEASPOON SIRACHA

½ TEASPOON ONION POWDER

1 TABLESPOON GARLIC POWDER

1 TBL RED WINE VINEGAR

OLIVE MAYO

1 CUP MAYO

1/2 CUP OLIVES **(EITHER BLACK OR GREEN OLIVES)**

½ TABLESPOON CAPERS

1 ANCHOVY

1 TEASPOON HERB DE PROVINCE

½ TEASPOON WHITE PEPPER

BLEND ALL INGREDIENTS IN FOOD PROCESSOR UNTIL SMOOTH.

SERVE AS A SPREAD ON A SANDWICH WITH COLD CUTS, LETTUCE, ONION AND TOMATO. OR EVEN IN POTATO SALAD.

ORANGE JULIUS DRESSING

2 CUPS ORANGE JUICE

1 CUP HEAVY CREAM

¼ CUP HONEY

1/8 CUP WHITE VINAGAR

1 TEASPOONSVANILLA

PUT IN POT AND REDUCE BY HALF. LET COOL AND REFRIGERATE.

CAN BE SERVED ON FRUIT SALADS, BEET SALAD.

PARSNIP PUREE

1 LB PARSNIPS PEELED AND CHOPPED INTO SMALL PIECES

1 SHALLOT SLICED THIN

3 CUPS WATER

1 TBL CHICKEN BASE

ADD PARSNIPS AND SHALLOTS TO WATER ADD CHICKEN BASE AND SIMMER UNTIL PARSNIPS ARE TENDER. APPROX 45 MINUTES. ADD PARSNIPS TO BLENDER WITH 1/2 CUP OF COOKING LIQUID AND 1/2 CUP OF HEAVY CREAM AND ½ TSP WHITE PEPPER AND PUREE UNTIL SMOOTH AND THICK.

THICKNESS SHOULD BE LIKE MASH POTATOES. IF NEEDED ADD SOME COOKING LIQUID IF NEEDED.

CHICKEN BASE YOU CAN FIND AT ANY GROCERY STORE.

CAN BE SERVED WITH CHICKEN, PORK, BEEF AND VEAL ON THE SIDE.

PEAR VINGARETTE

JUICE 2 PEARS AND PUT ON STOVE ON MEDIUM HEATAND REDUCE BY HALF

THEN REMOVE FROM STOVE AND COMBINE WITH THE REMAINING INGREDIENTS

2 OZS OF CHAMPAGNE VINGAR

6 OZS OF OLIVE OIL

1 MINCED SHALLOTS

1 TEASPOON HONEY

¼ TEASPOON KOSHER OR SEA SALT

¼ TEASPOON WHITE PEPPER

PUT ALL INGREDIENTS IN BLENDER AND BLEND UNTIL SMOOTH.

PEPPADEU KETCHUP

3 PEPPADEU PEPPERS **(CAN BE PURCHASED AT GROCERY STORES)**

3/4 CUPS MAYO

¾ CUPS KETCHUP

1/2 TEASPOON KOSHER OR SEA SALT

½ TEASPOON SIRACHA

PUT IN BLENDER UNTIL SMOOTH.

CAN BE SERVED AS A DIPPING SAUCE FOR SHRIMP, CRAB OR LOBSTER.

PICKLED YOGURT

2 CUPS PLAIN YOGURT

1 CUP DILL PICKLES AND ¼ CUP PICKLED **JUICE (ANY JAR PICKLES SWEET OR DILL)**

3 MINT LEAVES **(NO STEMS)**

1/8 TSP WHITE PEPPER

1/8 TSP SEA SALT

COMBINE ALL INGREDIENTS IN FOOD PROCESSOR UNTIL SMOOTH. STORE IN REFRIGERATOR.

CAN BE SERVED ON ANY LETTUCE OR FRUIT SALAD.

PIMENTO CHEESE

1/2 CUP CREAM CHEESE

1/2 CUP SHREDDED MOZZACLLA

1/2 TSP SCACHA

1/2 CUP SHREDDED CHEDDAR

¼ TSP WHITE PEPPER

¼ CUP MAYO

1/2 TSP ONION POWDER

1/2 TSP GARLIC POWDER

1/2 TBL OLIVE JUICE FROM BAR

1 ROASTED PEPPER

1 ANCHOVY

¼ CUP ROASTED TOMATOS FROM JAR

1/2 TSP SMOKED PAPIKA

BLEND ALL INGREDIENTS IN FOOD PROCESSOR LEAVE CHUNKY.

CAN BE USED AS A SPREAD WITH CHIPS, CRACKERS AND TOAST.

PISTACHIO SPICE MIX DIRT

1 TBL WHOLE CLOVE

1 TBL FENNEL SEED

1 TBL LAVENDER

1 WHOLE STAR ANISE

1 ½ QUARTS ROASTED PISTACHIOS

ROAST PISTACHIOS ON COOKY SHEET FOR 5 MINUTS AT 400 DEGREES

COMBINE ALL INGREDIENTS IN FOOD PROCESSOR UNTIL FINE DUST POWDER.

CAN BE SPRINKLED ON THE DISH WITH DUCK, STEAK OR FISH.

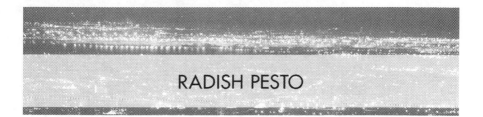

RADISH PESTO

3 ½ CUPS ARGULA

½ CUP RADISH SPROUTS

3 CLOVES GARLIC

¼ CUP PISTACHIOS

2/3 CUP BLENDED OIL

1 CUP PARM CHEESE

1 TEASPOON KOSHER OR SEA SALT

1 TEASPOON WHITE PEPPER

PUT ALL INGREDIENTS IN FOOD PROCESSOR. LEAVE CHUNKY.

SERVE ON ANY PASTA DISH OR TOP ON FISH

RICOTTA PESTO

2 CUPS RICOTTA

1/2 CUP PECANS

¼ CUP MAPLE SYRUP

½ TSP CINNAMON

¼ TSP SALT

¼ TSP WHITE PEPPER

1/2 TBL FINELY CHOPPED ROSEMARY

COMBINE ALL INGREDIENTS IN FOOD PROCESSOR UNTIL SMOOTH.

SERVE ON ANY PASTA OR AS A DIP WITH TOAST.

ROASTED GARLIC

TAKE GARLIC HEAD AND CUT THE THIN TOP OFF. PUT GARLIC ON ALUMIUM FOIL WITH THE TOP UP. SPRINKLE WITH OLIVE OIL SALT AND PEPPER. WRAP EACH GARLIC SEPERATELY IN ALUMIUM FOIL AND PLACE ON COOKIE SHEET.

PREHEAT OVEN TO 350 DEGRESS, PLACE COOKIE SHEET WITH GARLICS IN THE OVEN. COOK FOR 30 TO 40 MINUTES. REMOVE FROM OVEN AND LET COOL

THIS ROASTED GARLIC CAN BE COMBINED WITH MAYO FOR A ROASTED GARLIC MAYO.

THIS ROASTED GARLIC CAN BE WHIPPED WITH CREAM CHEESE FOR A CREAM CHEESE GARLIC SPREAD OR ANYTIME THE RECEIPES CALL FOR GARLIC.

ROASTED GARLIC DRESSING

1 CUP BUTTERMILK

2 CUPS MAYO

½ CUP GRATED PARM

JUICE AND ZEST OF 1 LEMON

2 ANCHOVIES

2 TEASPOONS OF BLACK PEPPER

1 TABLESPOON BALSAMIC VINAGAR

1 FULL CLOVE OF ROASTED GARLIC

COMBINE ALL INGREDIENTS IN BLENDER UNTIL SMOOTH

SAFFRON AIOLI

1/2 CUP WHITE WINE

1/2 TEASPOON SAFFRON THREADS

1 1/2 CUPS MAYO

DISSOLVE SAFFRON THREADS IN WHITE WINE OVER HEAT. LET COOL AND COMBINE WITH MAYO BY HAND.

CAN BE TOPPED OVER FISH, PORK.,MEAT OR PORK.

SALSA VERDE

1 CUP PARSLEY LEAVES **(NO STEMS)**

2 TEASPOONS CAPERS

½ CUP OLIVE OIL

2 ANCHOVIES

JUICE AND ZEST OF 1 LEMON

2 TABLESPOONS ROASTED GARLIC

2 TABLESPOONS DIJON MUSTARD

COMBINE ALL INGREDIENTS IN FOOD PROCESSOR AND LEAVE CHUNKY.

CAN BE USED OVER FISH, AND ALSO SERVED ON THE SIDE AS A CONDIMENT FOR ANYTHING.

SHERRY VINAIGRETTE

¼ CUP SHERRY VINEGAR

1 CUP OLIVE OIL

1 TABLESPOON SHALLOTS MINED FINELY

1 TEASPOON KOSHER OR SEA SALT

1 TEASPOON DIJON MUSTARD

PUT ALL INGREDIENRS IN BLENDER AND PUREE.

CAN BE USED AS A DRESSING FOR ANY GREENS, AND ALSO BEET SALADS.

SHRIMP COCKTAIL SAUCE

2 CUPS KETCHUP

JUICE OF 1 LEMON

2 TABLESPOONS HORSE RADISH

2 TABLESPOONS WORCESTERSHIRE SAUCE

2 TABLESPOONS TABACO SAUCE

½ TEASPOON KOSHNER OR SEA SALT

COMBINE ALL INGREDIENTS IN FOOD PROCESSOR AND LEAVE CHUNKY.

CAN BE USED WITH SHRIMP, CRAB, LOBSTER OR ANY OTHER SEAFOOD.

SMOKED POTATO SOUP

1 LB POTATOES- BOIL POTATOES IN SALTED WATER UNTIL THE INSIDE OF THE POTATO IS A LITTLE SOFT. DONOT PEEL POTATOES. COOL POTATOS DOWN IN COLD WATER THEN DRY THEM AND CUT IN HALF AND PUT THEM ON THE SCREEN PAN FACE DOWN.

SMOKE THE POTATOS IN A COLD OVEN FOR ABOUT 1 HOUR. WITH ANY SMOKE CHIPS YOU DESIRE.

PUT THE ITEMS BELOW IN A POT TO SIMMER UNTIL SOFTEN UP

1 ONION CHOPPED

1 LEEK CHOPPED

1 CELERY CHOPPED

ADD BUTTER AND COOK ABOVE ITEMS UNTIL SOFT

THEN ADD POTATOS

1 1/2 QUARTS OF WATER

2 TBL CHICKEN BASE

BRING EVERYTHING TO A BOIL AND COOK UNTIL POTATOS ARE SOFT. THEN ADD

3 TABLESPOONS MALT VINEGAR

2 TEASPOONS WHITE PEPPER

1 1/2 CUPS HEAVY CREAM

SIMMER FOR ABOUT 30 MINUTS THEN PUREE FINE. YOU CAN TOP THE SOUP WITH ANY OF THE DRESSINGS IN THIS BOOK THAT YOU DESIRE. ITS YOUR TASTE THAT MAKES THE SOUP.

SMOKED SALMON SAUCE

1 ½ CUPS CHOPPED SHALLOTS

¼ CUP BUTTER

COMBINE BOTH INGREDIENTS AND SIMMER UNTIL SHALLOTS ARE SOFT. WHEN SOFT PUT IN BLENDER

ADD THE FOLLOWING INGREDIENTS:

2 OUNCES PLAIN VODKA

¼ CUP GORGONZOLA CHEESE

1 CUP HEAVY CREAM

½ CUP BASIL LEAVES **(NO STEMS)**

½TEASPOON KOSHER OR SEA SALT

4 OUNCES SMOKED SALMON

COMBINE ALL INGREDIENTS IN FOOD PROCESSOR UNTIL SMOOTH. STORE IN REFRIGERATOR.

SERVE AS A TOPPING FOR THE SALMON, USE ALSO FOR CRAB, LOBSTER OR SEAFOOD SALAD

SMOKED MAYO

1 CUP MAYO

1 TEASPOON SMOKED PAPARIKA

1 TEASPOON CUMUN

BLEND ALL INGREDIENTS BY HAND.

SERVE ON SANDWICHS, FISH COCKTAILS, SHRIMP, CRAB AND LOBSTER COCKTAILS

SORRELL AIOLI

¾ CUP SORRELL HERB

1 CUP MAYO

1/2 TSP WHIT PEPPER

1 TSP KOSHER OR SEA SALT

1 ANCHOVIES

JUICE AND ZEST OF 1 LEMON

COMBINE ALL INGREDIENTS IN FOOD PROCESSOR UNTIL SMOOTH.

SERVE WITH SEAFOOD

SQUASH AIOLI

1 LARGE BUTTERNUT SQUASH

2 CUPS MAYO

½ TEASPOON ANY HOT SAUCE

½ TEASPOON KOSHER OR SEA SALT

½ TEASPOON WHITE PEPPER

CUT SQUASH IN HALF LENGTH WAYS AND REMOVE ALL THE SEEDS. PUT THE SQUASH FACE DOWN ON LINED COOKY SHEET AND RUB THE SKIN WITH OLIVE OIL. COOK AT 350 DEGREES UNTIL YOU CAN FEEL THE SKIN AND MEAT INSIDE BE SOFT.

REMOVE THE MEAT FROM THE SKIN AND PUT IN A FOOD PROCESSOR WITH THE REST OF THE INGREDIENTS. PROCESS UNTIL SMOOTH.

SERVE ON TOP OF DEEP FRIED CALIFLOWER OR BRUSSEL SPROUTS

SQUASH SOUP

1 ONIONS CHOPPED

1 ½ APPLES PEELED, SEEDED AND QUARTERED

2 ROASTED SQUASH

CUT SQUASH IN HALF LENGTH WAYS AND REMOVE SEEDS. PLACE SQUASH FACE DOWN ON PARCHMENT PAPER AND RUB SKIN WITH OLIVE OIL. COOK AT 350 FOR 1 HOUR OR UNTIL SQUASH IS SOFT. REMOVE MEAT FROM SKIN AND PUT ALL ABOVE INGREDIENTS IN A POT WITH 6 OZ OF BUTTER. COOK UNTIL ONIONS AND APPLES ARE SOFT. THEN ADD THE LAST TWO INGREDIENTS BELOW AND SIMMER FOR 1 HOUR MORE

ADD 1/2 QUART WATER

3 TABLESPOONS CHICKEN BASE

 BLENDER IN BLENDER UNTIL SMOOTH

TOP WITH MICRO GREENS AND BUTTERMILK SAUCE

STEAK SAUCE

2 SHALLOTS

20 CLOVES GARLIC

SAUTE IN BUTTER THEN ADD THE FOLLOWING

½ CUP COGNAC

½ CUP MADIERA

REDUCE BY HALF

PUT IN BLENDER AND ADD THE FOLLOWING

1 CUP DEMI GLAZE

1 TSP MUSTARD

¼ CUP ROASTED TOMATO

1 TBL BALSAMIC VINEGAR

1 TSP LIQUID SMOKE

¼ CUP WORCHESTICE SAUCE

1 TBL RED WINE VINEGAR

2 TBL BROWN SUGAR

2 TSP PORCINI POWDER

2 TSP SALT

1 TSP WHITE PEPPER

 BLEND ALL INGREDIENTS IN BLENDER UNTIL SMOOTH.

TOP THE STEAK WITH THE SAUCE

SWEET AND SOUR AIOLI

1 CUP MAYO

1/2 TEASPOON CUMUN

1/2 TEASPOON SMOKED PAPRIKA

1/2 TABLESPOON HONEY

BLEND ALL INGREDIENTS IN BLENDER UNTIL SMOOTH.

SERVE ON FISH, SEAFOOD COCKTAIL.

TAMARAND PESTO

½ CUP REAL MAPLE SYRUP

1 TSP WHITE SOY SAUCE

½ TSP GROUND GINGER

½ TSP GARLIC POWDER

1 TSP SESAME OIL

½ TSP SIRACHA

1 TBL TAMARAND CONCENTRATE **(CAN BE PURCHASED AT ANY GROCERY STORE)**

COMBINE ALL INGREDIENTS IN FOOD PROCESSOR UNTIL SMOOTH.

SERVE AS A DIP WITH TOASTED BREAD OR CRACKERS OR CHIPS.

TARTARE SAUCE

2 TSP HORSE RADISH

1 TSP DIJON MUSTARD

3 CUPS MAYO

JUICE AND ZEST OF 1 LEMON

1 TBL WORCESTERSHIRE

2 TBL OLD BAY SEASONING

1 TSP WHITE PEPPER

1 CUP PREPARED PICKLES WITH ONION AND GARLIC, AND A LITTLE JUICE. **(CAN BE BOUGHT AT ANY GROCERY STORE)(ANY JARRED PICKLES WILL DO)**

1 TSP HONEY

1 TBL HOT SAUCE

PULCE IN FOOD PROCESSOR LEAVE CHUNKY.

SERVE WITH ANY FRIED, BROILED OR BAKED FISH.

THAI CRAB BISQUE

1/2 CUP RED PEPPER CHOPPED

1/2 CUP ONION CHOPPED

1/2 CUP CELERY CHOPPED

SWEAT VEGETABLES IN 4 OZ BUTTER UNTIL SOFT. ADD 4 OZ FLOUR TO FORM A ROUG.

ADD

2 CANS OF 14 OZS COCONUT MILK

1 1/2 TABLESPOONS CRAB BISQUE

1/2 QUART MILK

JUICE AND ZEST OF 2 LIMES

1 CUP BASIL LEAVES

1 TEASPOONS RED CURRY PASTE

1/2 TABLESPOON WORESTERSHIRE

CONSTANTLY STIR THE CONTENTS ON THE STOVE UNTIL IT COMES TO A BOIL KEEP STIRRING FOR ABOUT 4 MINUTES AFTER IT COMES TO A ANOTHER BOIL PUT IN BLENDER BLEND SMOOTH.

SERVED WITH EITHER RED OR GREEN DEEP FRIED ONIONS.

TOASTED SESAME AIOLI

¼ CUP TOASTED SESAME SEEDS **(AVAILABLE IN GROCERY STORES)**

¼ CUP SESAME OIL

2 CUPS MAYO

1/2 TBL RICE WINE VINEGAR

COMBINE ALL INGREDIENTS IN FOOD PROCESSOR.

SERVED ON TOP OF ANY FISH THAT IS FRIED, BAKED. BROILED OR DEEP FRIED.

TRUFFLE MUSTARD VINEGARETTE

¼ CUP CHAMPAGNE VINEGAR

1 TSP DIJON MUSTARD

½ TSP SALT

¼ TSP WHITE PEPPER

¾ CUP OLIVE OIL

1 TABLESPOON TRUFFLE OIL **(PURCHASE AT ANY GROCERY STORE)**

MIX ALL INGREDIENTS BY HAND IN BOWL.

SERVE ON ANY GREENS FOR A SALAD OR MIX WITH MICRO GRENNS FOR TOPPING ON MEAT OR FISH, PORK OR VEAL.

VANILLA VINGARETTE

1 TABLESPOON VANILLA

1/2 CUP RED WINE VINEGAR

1/4 CUP SUGAR

1 CUP OLIVE OIL

1/8 CUP WATER

1/2 TEASPOON SALT

¼ TEASPOON WHITE PEPPER

COMBINE ALL INGREDIENTS IN BLENDER.

SERVE ON TOP OF BEET SALAD.

VERMOUTH CREAM

2 SLICES BACON CHOPPED

2 STUCKS CELERY CHOPPED

5 GARLIC CLOVES CHOPPED

1 SHALLOT CHOPPED

SAUTE ABOVE INGREDIENTS IN 4 OZ OF BUTTER UNTIL CARAMELIZED ABOUT 15 MINUTES. ADD ¾ CUPS OF FLOUR AND MAKE A ROUE THEN ADD THE FOLLOWING:

1/2 CUP VERMOTH

1 CUP JARED CLAM JUICE

2 1/2 CUPS WATER

1 TABLESPOON CHICKEN BASE

1 TABLESPOON CHOPPED TYME **(NO STEMS)**

1 TABLESPOON WORESTERSHIRE SAUCE

BRING TO BOIL AND SIMMER FOR ½ HOUR LET COOL PUREE IN FOOD PROCESSOR.

SERVE ON TOP OF ANY SEAFOOD DISH.

WASABI CRÈME FRAICHE

1/3 CUP WASABI POWDER-**(EQUAL AMOUNTS OF WATER AND WASABI) OR 2 TABLESPOONS WASABI PASTE.**

1/2 CUP MAYO

1/2 CUP CRÈME FRAICHE

1/2 TABLESPOON SALT

½ CUP BASIL LEAVES **(JUST LEAVES NO STEMS)**

PUREE IN BLENDER UNTIL SMOOTH

CAN BE SERVED ON FISH, MEAT, PORK, CHICKEN OR VEAL. OR WHERE EVER YOU LIKE.

WHITE BEAN AIOLI

1 CAN CANNALLINI BEANS

2 CUPS MAYO

1 TBL DIJON MUSTARD

1 TBL GARLIC POWDER

1 TSP WHITE PEPPER

1 TBL BALSAMIC VINEGAR

JUICE AND ZEST OF 1 LEMON

COMBINE ALL INGREDIENTS IN FOOD PROCESSOR UNTIL SMOOTH.

SERVE ON THE SIDE OR UNDERNEATH OF THE DISH WITH ROASTED PORK.

WING SAUCE

1/2 CUP SIRACHA

1/2 CUP ROASTED GARLIC PUREE

¼ CUP HONEY

ZEST AND JUICE OF 2 LIMES

COMBINE ALL INGREDIENTS WITH A WISK.

SERVE WITH ANY WINGS THAT YOU MAKE OR PURCHASE.

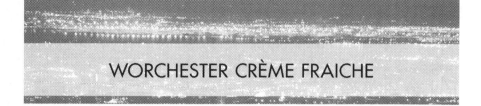

WORCHESTER CRÈME FRAICHE

1 CUP CRÈME FRAICHE

1/2 CUP MAYO

1/2 TABLESPOON ONION POWDER

1 TABLESPOON WORCHESTER SAUCE

1/2 TEASPOON KOSHER OR SEA SALT

½ TABLESPOON GARLIC POWDER

TO MAKE CRÈME FRAICHE: COMBINE 2 CUPS HEAVY CREAM AND 1/3 CUP BUTTERMILK LET SIT OUT OVERNIGHT UNTIL CREAMY. STORE IN REFRIGERATOR

COMBINE ALL INGREDIENTS IN BLENDER UNTIL SMOOTH.

SERVE AS A DIP FOR SHRIMP, CRAB MEAT, LOBSTER MEAT OR TOP ON ANY FISH EITHET FRIED OR BAKED.

LEMON VINGARETTE

3 OZS LEMON JUICE

3 GARLIC CLOVES

½ QUART EXTRA VIRGIN OLIVE OIL

½ TABLESPOON KOSHER OR SEA SALT

½ TABLESPOON WHITE PEPPER

MIX ALL INGREDIENTS IN BLENDER UNTIL SMOOTH.

USE **AS A SALD DRESSING ON GREENS, BEETS OR ANYOTHER SALAD.**

PANSZANELLA

1 LOAF OF DAY OR TWO OLD HARD CRUSTED ITALIAN BREAD

2 LARGE FRESH TOMATOES

1 MEDIMUM RED ONION CUT IN HALF AND THEN CUT IN THIN STRIPS

½ CUP EXTRA VIRGIN OLIVE OIL

3 TABLESPOON FRESH BASIL

½ TEASPOON KOSHNER OR SEA SALT

½ TEASPOON BLACK PEPPER

1 TABLESPOON BALSAMIC OR RED WINE VINEGAR

CUT UP ITALIAN BREAD INTO SMALL CUBES AND SOAK IN WARM WATER UNTIL SOFT. SQUEEZE THE WATER OUT OF THE BREAD AND PUT INTO A LARGE BOWL. CUT THE TOMATOES INTO ¼ INCH CUBES AND PLACE INTO THE BOWL. ADD THE RED THINNLY SLICED ONION, ADD SALT AND PEPPER. RIPE THE BASIL INTO PIECES DO NOT CUT WITH A KNIGE. ADD THE OLIVE OIL AND VINEGAR, MIX TOGETHER. IF IT FEELS DRY ADD MORE OLIVE OIL.

THIS CAN BE SERVED AS AN APPETIZER OR WITH SHRIMP COCKTAIL OR ANYOTHER APPETIZER OF YOUR CHOSING.

TRUFFLE BUTTER

1 LB UNSALTED BUTTER

2 TABLESPOONS TRUFFLE OIL

BRING BUTTER TO ROOM TEMPERATURE OR UNTIL VERY SOFT. COMBINE THE BUTTER AND THE TRUFFLE OIL IN A FOOD PROCESSOR AND BLEND UNTIL SMOOTH.

YOU CAN STORE THIS BUTTER ANYWAY YOU PREFER, IN A DISH, OR ROLL IT IN A LOG ON PLASTIC WRAP. STORE IN REFRIGERATOR.

CAN BE SERVE ON TOP OF ANY PREPARED FISH, PORK, STEAK OR VEAL CHOP

LOBSTER/SHRIMP POOR BOY DRESSING

1 CUP MAYO

JUICE OF 1 LEMON

3 TABLESPOONS GRAIN MUSTARD

1 TABLESPOONS SRIRACHA

½ RED ONION CHOPPED FINELY

1 TABLESPOON DILL CHOPPED FINE

COMBINES ALL INGREDIENTS IN BLENDER UNTIL SMOOTH.

CAN BE SERVED ON ANY SEAFOOD SANDWICH OR SEAFOOD COCKTAIL.

COLD SEAFOOD SALAD

1 LB SHRIMP PEELED AND DEVAINED

1 LB DIVER OR BAY SCALLOPS

½ LB MUSSELS

½ LB CLAMS **(CHERRY STONE CLAMS)**

½ LB CALAMARI BODIES

3 STALKS CELERY CUT IN SMALL PIECES

1 CUCUMBER PEELED SEEDED AND CUT IN SMALL PIECES

2 LEMONS

½ TEASPOON KOSHER OR SEA SALT

½ TEASPOON BLACK PEPPER

1 CUP EXTRA VIRGIN OLIVE OIL

DEBEARD THE MUSSELS THEN STEAM THE MUSSELS UNTIL THEY ALL OPEN UP IF SOME DO NOT OPEN DISCARD THEM, DO THE SAME WITH THE CLAMS. LET THE MUSSELS AND THE CLAMS COOL. STEAM THE SCALLOPS FOR ABOUT 10 MINUTES AND AGAIN LET COOL. STEAM THE CALAMARI FOR 10 MINUTES AND AGAIN LET COOL.

AFTER THE SEAFOOD HAS COOLED ARRANGE THE SEAFOOD IN A BOWL, ADD THE CELERY, THE CUCUMBERS ADD THE SALT AND PEPPER AND SQUEEZ THE LEMONS. ADD THE OLIVE OIL MIX AND COOL IN REFRIGERATOR.

CRAB SALAD

1 HEAD BOSTON SALAD

1 LB CRAM MEAT **(DOES NOT WHAT MATTER WHAT TYPE OF CRAB MEAT)**

1 CUCUMBER PEELED, SEEDED AND CUT IN SMALL PIECES

1 AVACOTO CUT IN HALF LENGTH WAYS REMOVE THE SEED REMOVE THE MEAT AND CUT IN SMALL PIECES

1/2 TEASPOON KOSHER OR SEA SALT

1/2 TEASPOON WHITE PEPPER

1 CUP SIRACHA MAYO

1 TABLESPOON PARSLEY CHOPPED

SIRACHA CONSIST OF 1 CUP OF MAYO AND 2 TABLESPOONS OF SIRACHA. SIRACHA IS A CHINESE HOT SAUCE CAN BE PURCHASED AT ANY GROCERY STORE.

ARRANGE LETTUCE IN A BOWL LIKE A CUP, ADD THE CRAB MEAT, CUCUMBER AND AVACOTO SPRINKLE WITH THE SALT AND PEPPER AND ADD THE MAYO. ADD THE PARSLEY

YOU CAN ADD LOBSTER MEAT IN SUBSTITUTE OF CRAK OR COOKED SCALLOPS.

DEEP FRIED CALIFLOWERS

1 HEAD CALIFLOWER CUT IN FLOWERETS

1 CUP FLOUR

½ TEASPOON KOSHER OR SEA SALT

½ TEASPOON BLACK PEPPER

½ CUP BACON **(CRISPY COOKED)**

½ CUP SQUASH AIOLI

¼ CUP HONEY

½ CUP PECANS

4 CUPS VEGTABLE OIL

 HEAT UP THE OIL TO 350 DEGREES ,TAKE TO CALIFLOWERETS OF CALIFLOWER AND DREDGE IN FLOUR REMOVE THE EXCESS FLOUR AND PUT INTO HEATED OIL FOR ABOUT 3 MINUTES. REMOVE AND ADD THE REST OF INGREDIENTS IN A BOWL WITH THE CALIFLOWER AND MIX.

YOU CAN SUBSTITUTE BRUSSEL SPROUTS OR BROCCILI

CHERRY TOMATO SAUCE

2 PINTS OF CHERRY TOMATOES

½ TABLESPOON KOSHER OR SEA SALT

½ TABLESPOON BLACK PEPPER

1 TEASPOON RED PEPPER FLAKES

1 TABLESPOON ROASTED GARLIC

1 AHCHOVY

½ TABLESPOON ORGANEO

½ CUP OLIVE OIL

TOSS CHERRY TOMATOES WITH OLIVE OIL, SALT, PEPPER & ORGANEO IN A LARGE BOWL AND SPREAD OUT ON COOKIE SHEET AND BAKE FOR 10 MINUTES AT 400 DEGREES.

PUT ALL INGREDIENTS IN FOOD PROCESSOR AND BLEND. LEAVE CHUNKY

SERVE ON ANY PASTA THAT YOU WANT

CHEESEBALL

4 OZ BUTTER

12 OZS CREAM CHEESE

1/2 CUP MAYO

1/2CUP CRÈME FRAICHE

1/2 TBL WORCHESTER SAUCE

1/2 TBL ONION POWDER

1/2 TBL DIJON MUSTARD

1/2 TSP KOSHER OR SEA SALT

1/2 TSP WHITE PEPPER

LET BUTTER AND CREAM CHEESE SOFTEN AT ROOM TEMPERATURE. WHEN SOFT COMBINE ALL INGREDIENTS IN FOOD PROCESSOR AND PROCESS UNTIL SMOOTH. REFRIGERATE IN A NICE BOWL. TO SERVE REMOVE FROM REFRIGERATOR ½ HOUR BEFORE SERVING. SERVE WITH CRACKERS OR ANY HARD CRUSTED BREAD OF YOUR CHOICE

SOME DIFFERENT SALAD IDEAS TO SERVE

ARUGLA SALAD

ARUGULA

GRAPES

RED ONION

BACON DRESSING

CANDIED PECANS

PEAR DRESSING

CAESAR SALAD

ROMAINE

FRIED EGG

FRIED ITALIAN SUSAGE

ROASTED GARLIC   DRESSING

BLUE CHEESE

TOMATO SALAD

ARUGULA

RED ONION

CHERRY TOMATOES

RED WINE VINAGAR DRESSING

EXTRA VIRGIN OLIVE OIL

BEET SALAD

COOKED BEETS

MIXED GREENS

THINLY SLICED RED ONIONS

GOAT CHEESE

FRENCH DRESSING

RISOTTO SALAD

ARUGULA

GRAPES

LEMON VINAGERETTE

MUSTARD MARMALADE

½ CUP ROASTED GARLIC

3 SHALLOTS SLICED VERY THIN

½ CUP RED WINE VINEGAR

½ CUP WATER

1 CUBE OF BEEF STOCK

2 TBL BROWN SUGAR

½ CUP MAYO

1 TABLESPOON DIJON MUSTARD

COOK THE FIRST 6 ITEMS IN SAUCE PAN FOR 45 MINUTES. LET COOL FOR AN HOUR. PUT IN BLENDER AND PUREE WITH 1/2 CUP OF MAYO AND 1 TABLESPOON OF DIJON MUSTARD.

SERVE WITH SHRIMP, CRAB OR LOBSTER COCKTAIL.

FENNEL AND MUSHROOM SALAD

1 BULB OF FENNEL CUT VERY THIN

2 CUPS MUSHROOMS CUT THIN (**RAW MUSHROOMS**) ANY TYPE IS FINE **REMOVE STEMS ON ALL MUSHROOMS**

¼ CUP SHALLOTS CUT VERY THIN AND SOAK IN WHITE VINEGAR FOR ABOUT 20 MINUTES

½ CUP SHAVED PIECES OF PARMISAM CHEESE **(TOP THE SALAD)**

½ TABLESPOONKOSHER OR SEA SALT

½ TABLESPOON WHITE PEPPER

3 TABLESPOONS LEMON PEEL **(YELLOW SKIN ONLY NO WHITE PITT)**

3 TABLESPOONS OF LEMON JUICE

½ CUP EXTRA VIRGIN OLIVE OIL

COMBINE ALL INGREDIENTS IN A BOWL, LESS THE CHEESE, SPRINKLE WITH SALT AND PEPPER ADD EXTRA VIRGIN OLIVE OIL. TOP WITH THE PARMISAM CHEESE.

GAZPACHO SOUP

2 LARGE TOMATOS

¼ RED ONION

1/2 RED PEPPER

2 GARLIC CLOVES

¼ CUP CUCUMBER

2 SLICES OF CRUSTY BREAD **(DAY OLD)**

1 TEASPOONS SALT

¾ TEASPOONS WHITE PEPPER

1/3 CUP SHERRY VINEGAR

2 CUPS OLIVE OIL

1 TEASPOONS SIRACHOR

PUT ALL INGREDIENTS IN THE BLENDER AND PROCESS UNTIL CHUNKY. SERVE COLD

BLUE CHEESE SAUCE

½ CUP SHALLOTS CHOPPED VERY FINE

3 TABLESPOONS UNSALTED BUTTER

3 TABLESPOONS REGULAR FLOUR

4 CUPS WHOLE MILK

½ TABLESPOON KOSHER OR SEA SALT

½ TABLESPOON WHITE PEPPER

2 CUPS CRUMBLED BLUE CHEESE

MIX ALL INGREDIENTS IN FOOD PROCESSOR AND STORE IN REFRIGERATOR. REHEAT WHEN DESIRED AND TOP ON ANY STEAK THAT YOU GRILLING OR PREPAREING ON THE STOVE.

SIRACHA MAYO

1 CUP MAYO

3 TABLESPOONS SIRACHA **(MAKE IT AS HOT AS YOU LIKE WITH THIS SAUCE)**

2 TABLESPOONS LEMON JUICE

½ TABLESPOON KOSHER OR SEA SALT

½ TABLESPOON WHITE PEPPER

PUT ALL INGREDIENTS IN BLENDER AND BLEND UNTIL SMOOTH. REFRIGERATE.

CAN BE SERVED AS A DIP FOR ANY SEAFOOD THAT YOU WANT.

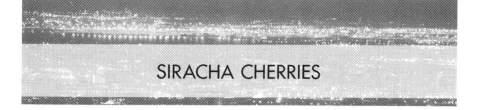

SIRACHA CHERRIES

1 1/2 CUPS CHERRIES

1 TSP SIRACHA

3 TSP CORN STARCH MIXED WITH 3 TSP COLD WATER

¼ CUP COLD WATER

PUT ALL INGREDIENTS IN SAUCE PAN EXCEPT FOR **CORN STARCH MIXTURE**

BRING INGREDIENTS TO A BOIL AND SLOWLY ADD CORN STARCH MIXTURE MIXING ALL THE TIME WHEN THICKEN REMOVE FROM HEAT AND LET COOL

SERVE ON TOP OF ANY PORK , STEAK, SEAFOOD OR VEAL DISH.

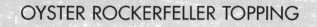

OYSTER ROCKERFELLER TOPPING

¾ CUPS MAYO

1 TABLESPOON CHOPPED GARLIC

2 TABLESPOONS PARMESAN CHEESE

1 TABLESPOON FRESH LEMON JUICE

1 TABLESPOON COGNAC **(ANY BRAND WILL DO)**

¼ TEASPOON KOSHER OR SEA SALT

¼ TEASPOON WHITE PEPPER

MIX ALL INGREDIENTS BY HAND AND STORE IN REFRIGERATOR UNTIL USED. TOP THE OYSTERS WITH COOKED SPINACH. COVER WITH THE SAUCE ON FRESHLY OPENED OYSTERS AND BAKE AT 400 DEGREES UNTIL TOPPING IS BUBBLING.

SUGGESTION IS TO ARRANGE THE OYSTERS TO BE COOKED ON A BED OF ROCK SALT ON A COOKIE SHEET.

BALSAMIC ONIONS

2 RED ONIONS PEELED AND CUT VERY THIN LENGTH WAYS

4 TABLESPOONS OF BALSAMIC VINEGAR

COOK ONIONS AND VINEGAR IN A PAN UNTIL IT IS REDUCED BY HALF. STORE IN REFRIGERATOR.

CAN BE TOPPED ON STEAKS, PORK CHOPS OR VEAL CHOPS

CANALLI BEAN PUREE

1 15.5 OZ CAN OF CANALLI BEANS

½ TABLESPOON KOSHER OR SEA SALT

½ TABLESPOON WHITE PEPPER

10 TABLESPOONS EXTRA VIRGIN OLIVE OIL

PUREE ALL INGREDIENTS IN BLENDER UNTIL SMOOTH. REFRIGERATE.

SERVED ON THE SIDE FOR PORK DISHES AND VEAL DISHES.

RASBERRY/MUSTARD SAUCE

1 CAN RED RASBERRIES

2 TABLESPOONS DIJON MUSTARD

2 TABLESPOONS SUGAR

½ TEASPOON EXTRA VIRGIN OLIVE OIL

½ TEASPOON SHERRY VINEGAR

PUT INGREDIENTS IN BLENDER AND BLEND FOR 1 ½ MINUTES. STORE IN REFRIGERATOR.

SERVE ON TOP OF PORK DISHES OR VEAL DISHES.

TOMATO FENNEL SAUCE

3 TABLESPOONS UNSALTED BUTTER

½ FENNEL BULB CUT IN QUARTERS

½ SWEET ONION PEELED AND CUT IN QUARTERS

5 GARLIC CLOVES PEELED

2 STALKS CELERY CHOPPED

1 JALEPENO SEEDED THEN CUT IN SMALL PIECES

½ TEASPOON KOSHER OR SEA SALT

½ TEASPOON WHITE PEPPER

½ CUP WHITE WINE

1 BOTTLE CLAM JUICE

(1) 15 OZ CAN OF PLUM TOMATOES

TAKE THE CAN OF PLUM TOMATOES AND BLEND IN A BLENDER UNTIL SMOOTH AND SET ASIDE. IN A LARGE SAUCE PAN MELT THE BUTTER THEN ADD THE CUT FENNEL, JALEPENO, ONION, GARLIC, CELERY, SALT AND PEPPER. COOK UNTIL EVERYTHING IS SOFT BUT NOT BROWN. ADD THE WINE AND CLAM JUICE AND REDUCE BY HALF. NOW ADD THE BLENDED TOMATOES AND COOK FOR ABOUT 15 TO 20 MINUTES. REMOVE FROM HEAT AND STRAIN AND STORE IN REFRIGERATOR.

SPINACH CRÈME FRISCH

1 BOX FROZEN SPINACH

2 CUPS CRÈME FRISCH

¼ TEASPOON KOSHER OR SEA SALT

¼ TEASPOON WHITE PEPPER

JUICE AND ZEST OF 1 LEMON

DEFROST THE SPINACH AND REMOVE EXCESS WATER BY SQUEEZING IT INTO A TOWEL OF CHEESE CLOTH.

COMBINE ALL INGREDIENTS IN FOOD PROCESSOR AND BLEND UNTIL SMOOTH. STORE IN REFRIGERATOR.